More TEAM BUILDING CHALLENGES

Daniel W. Midura, MEd
Roseville Area Schools
Roseville, Minnesota

Donald R. Glover, MS
White Bear Lake Area Public Schools
White Bear Lake, Minnesota

Human Kinetics

Library of Congress Cataloging-in-Publication Data

Midura, Daniel W., 1948-
    More team building challenges / Daniel W. Midura, Donald R. Glover
    p. cm.
    ISBN 0-87322-785-9
    1. Teamwork (Sports)   2. Physical education and training--Study
and teaching.   3. Team learning approach in education.   I. Glover,
Donald R.   II. Title.
GV706.8.M53   1995
796'.01--dc20   95-8965
                                                      CIP

ISBN: 0-87322-785-9

Acquisitions Editor: Richard D. Frey, PhD; **Developmental Editor:** Marni Basic; **Assistant Editor:** Susan Moore; **Editorial Assistant:** Alecia Mapes Walk; **Copyeditor:** Karen Bojda; **Proofreader:** Holly Gilly; **Graphic Artist:** Francine Hamerski; **Text Designers:** Robert Reuther and Keith Blomberg; **Cover Designer:** Jack W. Davis; **Photographer (cover):** Lorri Bettenga; **Photographers (interior):** Lorri Bettenga and Jim Cook; **Illustrators:** Dianna Porter and Craig Ronto; **Printer:** United Graphics

Human Kinetics books are available at special discounts for bulk purchase. Special editions or book excerpts can also be created to specification. For details, contact the Special Sales Manager at Human Kinetics.

Printed in the United States of America   10 9 8 7 6 5

Human Kinetics
Web site: **www.humankinetics.com**

United States: Human Kinetics, P.O. Box 5076, Champaign, IL 61825-5076
800-747-4457
e-mail: humank@hkusa.com

Canada: Human Kinetics, 475 Devonshire Road Unit 100, Windsor, ON N8Y 2L5
800-465-7301 (in Canada only)
e-mail: humank@hkcanada.com

Europe: Human Kinetics, P.O. Box IW14, Leeds LS16 6TR, United Kingdom
+44 (0) 113-278 1708
e-mail: humank@hkeurope.com

Australia: Human Kinetics, 57A Price Avenue, Lower Mitcham, South Australia 5062
(08) 82771555
e-mail: liahka@senet.com.au

New Zealand: Human Kinetics, P.O. Box 105-231, Auckland Central
09-309-1890
e-mail: humank@hknewz.com

More TEAM BUILDING CHALLENGES

To my friend Paul Busch—thank you for your guidance and encouragement over the years. And to my wife, Shirley—thank you for the first 25 years.

Dan Midura

To my beautiful wife and daughters, Carol, Chris, and Leigh.

Don Glover

Contents

Preface

Team building is fun, it is important, and it is gaining momentum. More and more classroom teachers, staff development coordinators, YMCA directors, recreational leaders, coaches, and physical educators are using team building techniques to enhance their programs and develop confidence in their program participants.

In our first book, *Team Building Through Physical Challenges*, readers were given 22 challenges ranging in difficulty from introductory to advanced. Many people who have used and enjoyed these challenges are asking for more. We trust the new challenges in this book will answer these requests.

These 15 new challenges, like the first ones, will give participants the opportunity to work together, struggle, deal with failure, and master the problems set before them. Team building offers an opportunity to build not just self-esteem in participants, but also better relationships among team members, confidence in others, and appreciation of the diversity of skills people bring into a group.

Some of the new challenges are our own creations, and some are the efforts of participants in our workshops. As part of our workshops, participants attempted to solve the 22 challenges in *Team Building Through Physical Challenges*, then they worked together to create new challenges. These new challenges show that it can be as enjoyable to create new tasks as it is to solve the challenges.

The activities in this book will require team members to interact verbally and physically in order to master the challenges. The skills of listening, encouraging, praising, receiving praise, and speaking clearly are integral parts of successful team building.

We feel strongly that our team building approach is more than just cooperative learning. We have built into each challenge specific points of accountability. Not all answers are correct. Participants have rules that must be followed. Sacrifices must be made if wrong responses occur. To be sure, there can be numerous ways to solve the challenges. But we want the participants to deal with something more than just the direct consequences of errors. They must also deal with a sacrifice, having to give up something for their mistakes.

We feel team building offers people the opportunity to look beyond self-centeredness. The skills learned in team-building activities can turn one from selfishness to selflessness. In turn, you should find that these new behaviors allow students to play games with a new focus. Games can be played for fun, the reinforcing of skills, the appreciation of one's teammates and opponents, or the appreciation of a good effort or performance, rather than just to win.

More Team Building Challenges will give teammates the joy of individual success but, more important, will reinforce the joy of the group in accomplishing a challenge by helping and depending on one another. These new team-building challenges are ideal for young children, athletes, adults, or anyone wishing to build closer relationships among team members.

We are excited about these new challenges. Try them. You and your students or team members will become a closer team, and you should find this enthusiasm spreading into other aspects of your program. In physical education circles we often hear the terms "lifetime sports" or "lifetime activities." Team building truly builds skills for a lifetime.

Acknowledgments

The authors wish to express their thanks to a number of people who helped create some of the challenges in this book.

Three challenges were conceived at a workshop held in La Crosse, WI.

Kim Baumgoldt, Armin Schwartz, Roger Knoblach, Tina Berry, Becky Rathke, Michelle Meyer, and Mary Ziegler helped to create Arachnohobia.

Diane Parr, Tammy Haay, Brian Kelly, Cathy Priteloft, Kathy Look, Mark Kiefler, and Anne Harris of the Intelligence Force created Team-A-Pod.

We adapted Raiders of the Lost Jewel from the challenge created by Nancy Jirsa, Dave LePesto, Lori Catlin, Konni Williams, Allie Brienzo, Eric Eswein, and Lorrae Swartz.

Knights of the Around Table was created at a workshop in Roseville, MN. Ron Long, Mike Nicholson, and Helen Seigal helped to create this challenge.

Ship to Shore was created at a workshop in Appleton, WI, by the Successful Seven: Kay Veldhorst, Jim Allman, Roger Young, Wendy Heckendorf, Christine Hart, Kathleen Leadley, and Dennis Giaimao.

Bridge Across the Amazon was adapted from the creation of the Mindful Doers of Appleton, WI: Karen Kerscher, Cindy Kolkema-Berndt, Sharon Jermstad, Eileen Hare, Dave Cepek, Mike Kleinhans, and Scott Arneson.

In addition, we thank Jean Ellingson for her help on word processing and Marni Basic for her editorial direction, and Jim Cook and Lorri Bettenga for taking photographs.

Chapter 1

What Is Team Building?

Failure is temporary; don't quit. Reorganize, renew, practice, and succeed!

As workshop leaders, we often ask our audiences, "What is team building?" Many people around the country have answered our question with the same answer: "Cooperative learning." In some aspects this answer is correct. In both cooperative learning and team building, students cooperate to solve a task. The similarity ends there. Cooperative learning and cooperative games are structured so that everybody wins and nobody loses. Cooperative games eliminate the fear of failing and make sure everyone becomes a winner.

Team building strives to teach that failure is only temporary and that when one fails, reorganization and renewed efforts are needed. Team-building enthusiasts realize that failing along the way can build a much sweeter path to success. Team building requires that certain rules be kept and that if the rules are broken, consequences must be suffered or sacrifices made. Team building puts a premium on the relationships between teammates; what counts is not if the team solves the challenge, but how the team works together to eventually solve the challenge.

Some physical educators believe team building will replace competition within our traditional curriculum. Nothing could be further from the truth. We believe that competition is inherent in our curriculum; however, kids need techniques to learn how to better handle the stresses of competition. Team building is not attempting to replace competition but only to enhance it by teaching children to become better teammates.

Building a Positive Self-Concept

Success depends on a lot of factors; a primary one is self-concept. Self-concept is largely developed by how others perceive us and react to our efforts. If we receive positive reactions, our social development flourishes, and we have a better chance to succeed.

Self-confidence grows as physical challenges are successfully mastered. As we build self-confidence and succeed at progressively harder challenges, we feel better about ourselves and our abilities. With a positive self-concept, one can overcome failures and eventually gain success. A positive self-concept gives a person courage to try.

Physical challenges offer a process that builds self-confidence for both individuals and groups. When a person's effort helps a group accomplish its goal, that person is accepted as an integral part of a winning team. As the concept of belonging to a successful team develops, each person takes an active role rather than being a passive observer. Teammates learn that the cooperative process is what is important—winning becomes a by-product.

Figure 1.1 Team building will help students learn how individual efforts combine to help the team accomplish goals.

Physical Education's Role in a Child's Development

Many physical educators believe that team building may replace physical education's main thrust: that of building fitness and skills in our students. On the contrary, we believe that fitness and skill development should remain physical education's main goal. We also believe physical education helps develop a child's cognitive ability. Children learn to think on their feet, make quick decisions, and understand rules and strategies. Many of us were taught in college that physical education helps a child socially and emotionally, and many of us didn't question this. We figured if kids were put on a team and played in the many games and contests that our curriculum offers, they would grow socially and emotionally. But merely putting children into competitive situations is not enough. Is there more we can do to foster that social and emotional growth? Can we teach kids how to fail and succeed—teach them to become good teammates and help foster their self-esteem? Yes, we can, through the technique of team building.

Creating Success Experiences

A success experience in team building doesn't mean just scoring a touchdown or kicking a goal. A success experience might be contributing an idea or having teammates listen to your plan. We all feel good about ourselves when we can influence the direction of a group. All students in physical education need the opportunity to establish relationships so they feel like part of a group. This success experience should permeate physical education and sports. Sometimes only a talented few gain the success experience of recognition for their accomplishments, but everyone involved in team building will attain this reward.

One of the most important success experiences all students have a right to achieve is fun. Students should have fun through play, leave the gym with smiles, and look forward to coming back for more fun.

The Teacher's Role in Team Building

Please don't believe that physical challenges create false self-confidence. Children know when something is given to them and when something is earned. We all know that when we earn something, we take great pride in its ownership. Your team builders should not be allowed to complete a challenge until they truly earn it. Allow failure and struggle. Allow conflict and resolution. Team builders will only improve if they work hard and master a challenge they perceive to be difficult.

Physical educators must be ready to accept responsibility in areas other than skill development in the future. We must contribute to the development of thinking skills and social responsibility. Physical education must win a position of respect alongside other academic offerings. Team building can add to our recognition and respect. Team building is a strategy for the future, and physical educators can be leaders in promoting this concept.

Chapter 2

Getting Organized

Being able to praise someone is a skill that needs to be encouraged.

Before students are actually placed on a team or before a team attempts any challenges, kids will need to know what makes a good teammate. They should know that the more confidence each teammate has in his or her team, the harder the team will work to solve a challenge.

Encourage Praise

One way to raise the confidence level of one's teammates is praise. Everyone likes to know when his or her efforts are appreciated and recognized. Students take a risk when they praise a teammate—they may not be used to praising each other, or they may be bashful. Whatever the case, they need practice using this skill. We make students practice physical skills; why shouldn't we make them practice saying nice things?

A list of praise phrases appears on page 7. Copy and laminate this sheet. Give each student a copy, and read through the phrases together. Think of some new praise phrases and list them. Encourage your students to use specific praise phrases during a challenge attempt. Most important, be an example; use praise phrases appropriately while your students are working on challenges. Students will learn how to use praise phrases by watching and listening to you. You will find that you enjoy your day much more if you spend it praising your students for their hard work!

Discourage Negative Pressure and Put-Downs

Once students know that praise and encouragement will help a team move toward challenge completion, they should also recognize what hinders that progress. Explain to them what a put-down is, and point out that any attempt to make someone feel bad will harm the whole team. "Chris, we don't want you on our team. You can't do anything!" is a specific and deliberate attempt to harm Chris. To be good teammates, children should know that encouraging and helping a teammate will ultimately help the whole team.

Negative pressure is also something children should recognize and try to eliminate from the team. A frown or an impatient look can send a negative message and put undue pressure on an anxious teammate. Try to demonstrate examples of put-downs and negative pressure so that your students can recognize and soon stop using these harmful techniques and behaviors.

Praise Phrases

Praise and encouragement are two ways we can all feel good about the team. Here are 25 ways to say "Very good!" Copy and laminate this list, or create your own.

1. "Good for you!"
2. "You did that very well."
3. "Couldn't have done it better myself."
4. "You're doing fine."
5. "Now you've figured it out."
6. "Outstanding!"
7. "Good work."
8. "You figured that out fast."
9. "You did well today."
10. "Nice going."
11. "You're getting better every day."
12. "You're learning fast."
13. "You make it look easy."
14. "You did a lot of work today!"
15. "Keep it up!"
16. "Nice job."
17. "That's really nice."
18. "That's great."
19. "Way to go!"
20. "That's the way to do it!"
21. "Good thinking."
22. "Keep up the good work."
23. "That's the right way to do it."
24. "You remembered!"
25. "I've never seen anyone do it better."

Use Positive Adjectives

Once students have attempted three or four challenges as a team, they are ready to try positive adjectives. The team should sit in a semicircle. Give each team member a list of positive adjectives to use to describe personal characteristics of other team members. A list of positive adjectives appears below.

Positive Adjectives

Kind	Enthusiastic
Strong	Helpful
Nice	Convincing
Happy	Bright
Active	Thoughtful
Cheerful	Courteous
Content	Polite
Sensible	Intelligent
Friendly	Creative
Energetic	Independent
Organized	Determined
Courageous	Humorous
Honest	Pleasant
Clever	Delightful
Inventive	Confident
Imaginative	Daring

One by one, each team member moves to the front of the semicircle and faces the teammates. Each teammate in turn picks three positive adjectives to describe the teammate sitting in the front of the semicircle. The speaker should look at the person in the center, say that person's name, and use the three adjectives. For example, "Chris, you are smart, kind, and happy." This may produce giggles at first, but students find that we all enjoy hearing something nice being said to us. This exercise gives each teammate an opportunity both to praise others and to be praised. This positive adjective exercise does not have to be used after each challenge. Use it once or twice every few challenge   s the group develops team-building skills, you may choose to eliminate this activity.

Organize the Challenges

The teacher should assign the teams. Six to nine members on a team works best. Once all students are on a team, let each group pick a team name. Make sure the names selected are positive. Don't accept a name like the "Brainless Bunch."

Encourage the team to select a positive name like the "Brainy Bunch" or the "Magnificent Minds."

Students' Roles

Once the teams are organized and named, it is time to give some of the team members more responsibility. Roles are assigned to team members. These roles should rotate among team members with every challenge. These roles are described in the following sections. Not all roles need to be filled each time. The organizer, however, always needs to be appointed.

Organizer

The organizer helps team members understand the challenges (see Figure 2.1). As each task begins, the organizer will receive two cards: an organizer card and a challenge card. These cards are integral parts of each challenge because they are the only sources of information for group members. Give a copy of each card to the organizer before a challenge begins. (These cards can be found in Appendix B. Please copy and laminate each card.)

The challenge card lists the equipment, the starting position, the challenge, and the rules and sacrifices for each challenge. A sacrifice is a consequence of breaking a rule. For instance, it may mean that one successful challenge solver or the entire team must start the challenge over from the beginning.

Figure 2.1 With the organizer's help, all team members should understand the challenge before they start.

The organizer card lists questions the organizer will ask team members to help them understand each challenge. A team cannot start a challenge until it can answer all the questions correctly. After the team answers the questions, the challenge begins. The instructor enforces the rules on the organizer card.

If the group becomes stumped while trying to solve the challenge, the organizer can ask the instructor for tips. Remember, though, that by giving too much help you defeat the purpose of problem solving. Let the team go as far as it can before you step in to help.

Praiser

We hope everyone in the group will use praise phrases. But the praiser is assigned the task of finding specific acts to praise, which are identified after the completion of the challenge.

Encourager

An encourager also acknowledges effort, and many times this role overlaps that of the praiser. An encourager must use positive encouragement while a teammate is attempting a challenge. The encourager's job is continuous while the task is underway. Again, we hope everyone on the team will be encouraging.

Summarizer

After each challenge, the summarizer will tell the instructor how the team solved the challenge, what was fun for the team, what was hard, and how to improve the task. After all the teams have completed a specific challenge, the summarizer can tell the class how their team solved the challenge. The summarizer should have a team report card. (An example can be found in Appendix A. Make a copy and laminate it.)

Recorder

The recorder highlights for the class specific praises and encouragement used during the challenge.

Instructor's Responsibilities

The instructor needs to avoid solving the challenges. It is very tempting to help each team, but members need to learn how to function when things become difficult. Let them struggle. Allow them to fail before giving in to an organizer's request for help.

When setting up equipment, use all available safety precautions, including plenty of mats. Study the figures in this book and know where to place mats. Discourage horseplay or unsafe behavior.

Be a good observer, encourager, and praiser. Do everything possible to eliminate negative team pressure.

Be ready to adapt the challenges when necessary, but enforce rules and sacrifices. Don't be afraid to be creative. You don't have to use an organizer card to describe a challenge, although we feel they play a useful role in these tasks. Use your imagination. For instance, if you want to put a time limit on the Grand Canyon II activity (see chapter 5), you could say "Okay, Magnificent Minds, your task is to get everyone from this cliff to the other cliff before the storm hits in 15 minutes. You are stranded on this cliff and one of your members is injured. The only way your team can get to the other cliff and down the mountain is by swinging across the canyon on this vine." Don't hesitate to place alligators in the water, storms on the horizon, or other hazards that make a challenge more interesting.

Yearly Organization

As we have said, challenges fit into the curriculum in many ways. We find that beginning a school year with a few challenges sets a positive atmosphere in the class that carries over into later units of study. After fall outdoor units, you can do a few more challenges. After a few months of indoor winter activities, students are eager to try more challenges. You will find that the cooperation and teamwork learned in the challenges carry over into your established curriculum.

Another way to present the challenges is as a unit. Try to include as many challenges as possible within a 1- or 2-week time span. However you present the challenges, you will find them popular with students.

Class Organization

Here are two ways to present the challenges: Set up one challenge for all groups, or set up several challenges and let teams rotate. If you select the second method, make sure you have enough equipment.

If you set up five or six challenge stations in your gym and your class has three or four groups, you will always have challenge stations open to receive the next group.

If a team does not finish a challenge, let them try again the next class period. A team may need up to three class periods to finish a challenge.

Gym Setup

We have chosen five challenges to illustrate a gym setup:

- Skywriters (chapter 3)
- Grand Canyon II (chapter 5)
- Knights of the Around Table (chapter 5)
- The Swamp Machine (chapter 3)
- Island Escape (chapter 4)

These challenges range from introductory to advanced. As you can see from Figure 2.2, the five challenges are spaced around the gymnasium with ample room at each station. Teams rotate to an open station after completing a challenge.

These five challenges will provide activity for an average-sized class of 24 to 42 students, with 6 to 10 group members on a team. Try to leave the equipment up

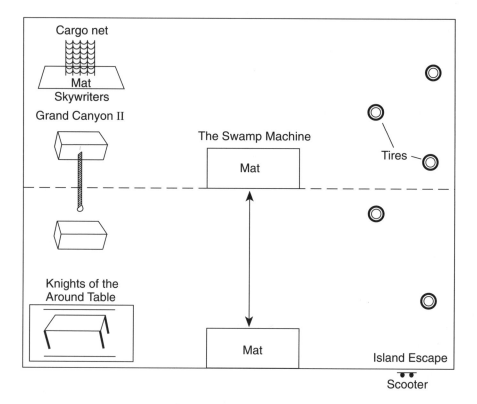

Figure 2.2   Example of gym setup showing materials for Skywriters, Grand Canyon II, Knights of the Around Table, The Swamp Machine, and Island Escape.

for several days so all teams can rotate without having to move the equipment each day.

If teams are kept together, the positive adjective exercise is not necessary after each challenge. It's best, in fact, to keep groups together for at least a week so they can develop team-building skills with familiar teammates. If you change teammates, use positive adjectives more frequently.

Adaptations for Special Children and Situations

Mainstreaming means more children with physical and mental disabilities are entering physical education classrooms. Team building is an excellent way to mainstream these students into group activities. Can you imagine how children with special needs feel when they accomplish a physical challenge? Can you imagine how a group feels when it helps a special person accomplish a challenge?

Use good judgment and understand that not all children with disabilities can accomplish every task. Involve special students as much as possible, but modify each task by providing rest areas, shorter distances, and additional physical help from team members. Allow special students to struggle, to work with the team to solve the task, and to fail. Having a child with special needs in a group can enhance the teamwork lesson.

Resolving Conflicts

Children, like adults, have personality conflicts. Some are aggressive and domineering. Some may not bathe regularly. Counseling may be necessary, but we have found that during team building, personality conflicts diminish. You, as team builder, should ensure that students don't badger or tease each other.

Teacher, Prepare Thyself

Use the Instructor Preparation Form in Appendix A to review the challenges you use. It serves as a quick reference while you are in the gymnasium or work area.

Safety First

Review the safety notes for each challenge, and add the safety measures necessary for your gym or groups.

Getting Started

Now you're ready to start the physical challenges. We recommend that you start with easier challenges and progress to advanced tasks as team building strengthens. Introductory, intermediate, and advanced challenges are detailed in the next three chapters.

Before you begin, remember some important concepts:

1. Safety first. If you have an open area on the floor, mat it. Don't let imagination overrule common sense. If you don't think a challenge is safe, either don't do it or make it safer.
2. Adjust heights, distances, obstacles, and difficulty to match your students' developmental levels.
3. Be positive, enthusiastic, and encouraging. Teach your students to be the same. Remind them to use praise phrases and positive adjectives after selected challenges.

We hope you will enjoy the physical challenges. We know your students will love and look forward to them.

Chapter 3

Introductory Challenges

Team building is an excellent way to mainstream children with physical and mental disabilities into group activities. Imagine how children with special needs feel when they accomplish a physical challenge. Imagine how the group feels when they help a special child accomplish a challenge.

The Great Communicator

Violence in our schools and society is a growing concern for all of us. Doesn't it make sense that if students learn to praise, to compliment, and to become effective team members, then progress toward violence prevention can be made?

The Great Communicator is a very important challenge if you want to use the challenges to really build teamwork. Even though it is not a physical challenge like the others, it is essential for developing listening skills. If group members do not listen to one another, how can they communicate ideas? Group members also need practice speaking to one another so that they can clearly explain the ideas they wish to put into action. You can have all your groups try the Great Communicator at one time. Space is not an issue. This challenge can be done in a classroom or a gymnasium.

We suggest you try this challenge early in your team-building program. As your groups develop (or struggle to develop), you may wish to repeat this challenge from time to time as a test of communication success.

Description

The group members sit either in a semicircle or randomly in an area assigned only to that group. One member of the group is selected as the Great Communicator (see Figure 3.1).

Figure 3.1 Working the Great Communicator challenge.

The Great Communicator attempts to describe a picture in terms that will allow the group members to draw the objects being described. The Great Communicator may not, however, use certain terms describing standard shapes. Terms such as circle, square, rectangle, or triangle may not be used. Also, group members may not ask the Great Communicator questions or request further descriptions.

We suggest that you give the task of Great Communicator to a different group member after each picture is completed.

Success Criteria

Unlike our other challenges, we have not defined criteria for success. The group members will show their group the completed pictures after the Great Communicator has completed his or her description. The group will be able to observe if they, as individuals or as an entire group, understood the descriptions given.

Equipment

Each group member will need a pencil and one piece of paper per drawing. You will need to give each Great Communicator a picture to describe (see Appendix A or make up your own). A clipboard should be used by the Great Communicator so that the group members cannot see through the page he or she is using.

Setup

The only setup necessary is to give the group members the necessary equipment and to allocate a working space of a 10-foot circle or square for each group.

Rules and Sacrifices

There are no sacrifices for this task. The Great Communicator is not allowed to use the designated terms for shapes.

Possible Solutions

The solutions to this challenge will vary according to the descriptive skills of the Great Communicator and the listening skills of the group members. The purpose of this challenge is to give group members an opportunity to practice communication skills. As they display their drawings and compare them to the Great Communicator's picture, they will get an indication of their success in listening and speaking. As the group practices this challenge a few times, members should see an improvement in their communication efforts and skills.

Conclusion of the Task

The task is completed when the Great Communicator has finished describing the picture. The group members will show their finished drawings to the Great Communicator and to each other.

Additions and Variations

Feel free to use the picture examples we have given in Appendix A. As you use this challenge, you or your students can supply your groups with additional or more creative examples to describe.

Caution: Construction Zone

In many present-day games and sports, decisions and activity are dominated by those who are most aggressive or most athletically inclined. In team building, everyone participates in the decisions, and everyone has to be included in the activity in order for the group to succeed.

Like the Great Communicator, Caution: Construction Zone is more a communication challenge than simply a physical challenge. Some group members, using verbal clues and cues, will assist other group members (the construction workers), who will be wearing blindfolds, to assemble a large puzzle. The challenge is not only for the blindfolded group members to complete the puzzle, but also for the sighted group members to communicate in a clear manner so that the construction workers can successfully follow the directions given to them.

Description

You can have as many of the group members blindfolded as you wish. Of course, at least one group member must remain sighted. For our discussion, let's assume three or four group members are blindfolded.

After blindfolding the designated construction workers, the sighted group members mix up the parts of the puzzle. Although there is no end to the types of puzzles you or your students could create, we assume the puzzle you will use will become a square when assembled.

The sighted group members give verbal directions to the blindfolded construction workers. The construction workers will need to be guided to the puzzle pieces and then be guided in assembling them. The sighted groups are not allowed to touch the puzzle pieces or the blindfolded group members.

We suggest you make your working area completely free of obstructions or other physical structures.

Success Criteria

This challenge is mastered when the puzzle is correctly assembled.

Equipment

You will need one to four blindfolds plus a construction puzzle (see Figure 3.2 for an example). The puzzle could be made from 4-by-4-foot, 1/4-inch plywood or even tag board. We recommend the puzzle pieces be color-coded on one side so students know which side should face up.

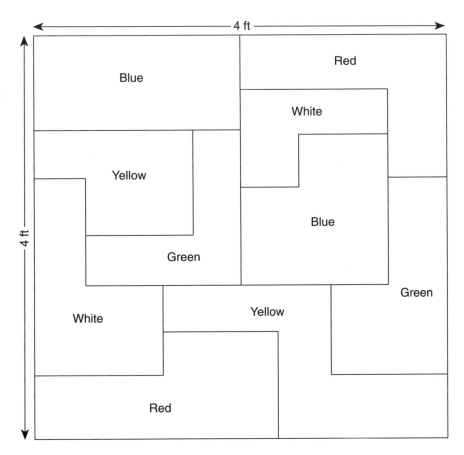

Figure 3.2 A construction puzzle used in Caution: Construction Zone. Puzzle pieces should be painted on one side to make the challenge easier.

Setup

This challenge does not require a great deal of space. The task could be done in a classroom, hallway, or gymnasium. A 10-by-10-foot area with no obstructions is adequate.

Rules and Sacrifices

1. Only the blindfolded team members may touch the puzzle pieces. If sighted members physically touch puzzle pieces, the group must mix up the puzzle again and start from the beginning.
2. The sighted group members may not physically touch the blindfolded group members. The same sacrifice as in rule 1 applies.
3. No one may use put-downs or last names.

Possible Solutions

The solution to the task is simply to assemble the puzzle. The level of difficulty will depend on the verbal skills of the sighted group members and the manipulative skills of the blindfolded construction workers (see Figure 3.3). Of course, you can increase the level of difficulty by providing more difficult puzzles.

Figure 3.3 Assembling the construction puzzle.

Conclusion of the Task

When the puzzle has been assembled, the blindfolded group members will remove their blindfolds.

Additions and Variations

You may wish to put a time limit on each construction group. You could tape an outline of the puzzle onto the floor to help the group in the construction process. We suggest that you either have the group rebuild the puzzle with new blindfolded members or provide the group with a new puzzle so that all the group members take a turn as blindfolded construction workers.

Note. Using large puzzles seems to be more motivating for the people involved in the task as well as more interesting for others observing the challenge.

The Riverboat

Decision making during team building is a team process for systematically selecting among alternative solutions. Ideally, this will reinforce everyday problem-solving skills for each member of the team.

The Riverboat is an introductory challenge requiring a group to transport themselves across a large open space. There is one basic solution to this task, but it usually takes a group the better part of a class period to successfully complete the challenge.

Description

The team will transfer themselves from one end of a basketball court-sized area to the other end without touching the floor with their bodies. The group uses two folded tumbling mats to create a riverboat. The mats must be moved in such a manner that they do not come unfolded. The mats also must not crash onto the floor making a loud noise.

Success Criteria

The Riverboat challenge is mastered when all the group members have successfully crossed the gym space (the river) without touching the floor with their bodies. All the assigned equipment must be brought to the opposite side of the river as well.

Equipment

You will need two standard-sized tumbling mats, two small tires (preferably boat trailer tires) and two long jump ropes or sash cords (see Figure 3.4).

Figure 3.4 The Riverboat equipment.

Setup

You will need a long open space the length of a standard basketball court. A wide hallway would also provide an adequate work space.

Rules and Sacrifices

1. If a group member touches the floor with any part of the body, the entire group must go back to the starting position.
2. All the equipment must be brought across the river.
3. The mats must remain folded. If they unfold, the entire group returns to the starting position.
4. If a mat crashes to the floor and makes a loud noise, the group must start again.
5. No one may call a teammate by his or her last name.

Possible Solutions

Generally, the group places one mat on the floor and then passes the other mat to the front. The group members move to the front mat, then they lift, pass, or slide the other mat to the front. Next they transfer to the new front mat and repeat the process in a leap-frog manner (see Figure 3.5). Often, they use the tires as "lifeboats" or "tugboats" to assist in the passing of the tumbling mats. The tires also reduce crowding on the riverboat. The jump ropes are usually tied to the tires in order to move them more efficiently.

Figure 3.5 Carrying out the Riverboat challenge.

Conclusion of the Task

The challenge is completed when the group has successfully crossed the river and has brought all the equipment with them.

Additions and Variations

You may wish to make this task more difficult by creating obstacles in the river or requiring a portage to take place. You might want to create a storm story so that the group must reach certain points within a time limit.

The Swamp Machine

Team building produces greater commitment and higher quality work.

Team building ensures everyone will be treated with dignity and respect.

Team building produces a challenging environment that produces a spirit of inquiry, expression of creativity, and positive risk taking.

Team building produces mutual respect, caring relationships, and acceptance of differences. This, in turn, promotes positive growth for everyone.

Philosophy of White Bear Lake Schools
White Bear Lake, MN

The Swamp Machine challenge requires group members to transport themselves across a defined space using a tumbling mat. The tumbling mat will need to have its Velcro ends attached so that the mat forms a ring that the group members can get inside of and roll like the tracks of a military tank. We will describe this task using a 6-by-12-foot UCS mat with 1-foot segments. Other mats can be used; see the section on variations.

Description

The group members will begin on one side of the gym at a designated island (two unfolded tumbling mats, side by side). Two to four group members will get into the swamp machine and maneuver it across the swamp to the other island. Some of the group members will then get out of the swamp machine. At least two group members must remain in the swamp machine as it travels back across the swamp to pick up more group members. Group members will have to trade places often as there must always be two to four members in the machine as it travels back and forth across the swamp. No group member may take more than two consecutive trips across the swamp. The group continues the challenge until all the group members have successfully crossed the swamp to the second island.

Success Criteria

The Swamp Machine challenge will be mastered when all the group members are standing on the second island and the swamp machine is parked on shore.

Equipment

You will need four standard tumbling mats to create two islands (two mats each, side by side). We recommend a 6-by-12-foot UCS tumbling mat with 1-foot segments (most standard mats are made in 2-foot segments) and Velcro ends that can be attached together for the swamp machine.

Setup

Place two unfolded, standard tumbling mats, side by side to create an island. Place the other two mats in a similar fashion approximately 30 to 40 feet away (about one half the length or the full width of a basketball court) to create a second island. Any long open space, such as a hallway or cafeteria, would be sufficient for this challenge. Place the swamp machine on the first island with its Velcro ends attached together.

Rules and Sacrifices

1. If a group member touches the floor (swamp), that person and one successful person must go back to the first island.
2. If the swamp machine falls apart, there is no sacrifice if the group members inside repair it while it is in the swamp. If the group members inside the swamp machine cannot repair it while it is in the swamp, the entire group must return to the first island.
3. No group member may take more than two consecutive trips across the swamp. If one does, that person plus one person from the second island must go back to the first island.
4. There must always be from two to four group members in the swamp machine as it crosses the swamp. If there are fewer than two or more than four, the entire group must start the challenge again from the beginning.
5. No last names or put-downs may be used.

Possible Solutions

Generally, the group members will get inside the swamp machine on the first island and roll it forward to the other island (see Figure 3.6). One or two of the group members will get out of the machine, stand on the second island and send the machine back to the starting area. The swamp machine may veer off to the side if the group travels too fast or if they do not work carefully together. As the group goes back and forth, they need to make sure the Velcro ends stay together. They should check the ends after each trip.

The group members need to mathematically determine some of their sequences so that they do not leave certain group members stranded as the challenge nears completion. Group members may reach the second island thinking they are done with the task, only to find that they need to get back into the machine to retrieve other teammates.

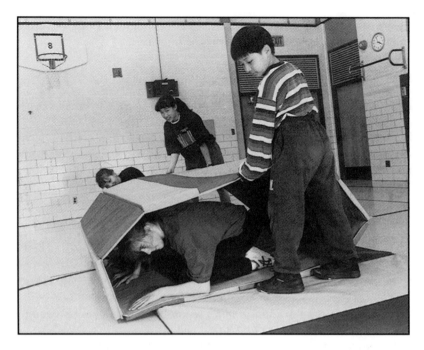

Figure 3.6 Carrying out the Swamp Machine challenge.

Conclusion of the Task

All the group members will be standing on the second island with the swamp machine parked on shore when the task is concluded.

Additions and Variations

You may wish to create a story sequence, such as "A storm is approaching... You have 10 minutes to get your group to safety on the other shore." You may wish to challenge the group to get their teammates across the swamp in fewer than four moves.

   If you do not have a mat like the one we described (a 1-foot-segmented mat, such as those manufactured by UCS), you may wish to attach two standard tumbling mats together. Make sure the Velcro ends hold together well.

Skywriters

Remember: students say to themselves, "in order to participate, I must fit in."

The Master Teacher, Inc.
Manhattan, KS

Skywriters is a challenge that uses a hanging cargo net. Group members will attempt to build a series of shapes or patterns on the cargo net using the bodies of all the group members to form each figure. If you do not have a cargo net, you can simply modify a few directions so that the students can create the same patterns on the floor or on mats covering the floor. Skywriting on a cargo net is physically demanding. Skywriting on the floor would be appropriate for younger students.

Description

Group members will build a series of shapes or patterns. Group members begin by standing on the mats under the cargo net. All the members must climb onto the cargo net to form the shape. After each shape is approved, all the group members must get off the cargo net before the next shape is constructed. Using paper and pencils, the group can prepare a plan whereby each person is assigned a specific part of the designated shape. The group can be given a checklist of specific shapes from which to choose their skywriting, or you can have them create their own assignments. A sample checklist has been provided in Appendix A.

Success Criteria

Using all its members, the team will construct a designated number of shapes from the checklist provided to them. The challenge will be mastered when all the shapes have been constructed and approved by the teacher. We suggest a minimum of six shapes be constructed. If you are using a cargo net, all the shapes must be created on the net.

Equipment

The necessary equipment includes a cargo net, mats or crash pads under the net for safety, a checklist of shapes to be built, plus paper and pencils for drawing and preparing plans (see Figure 3.7).

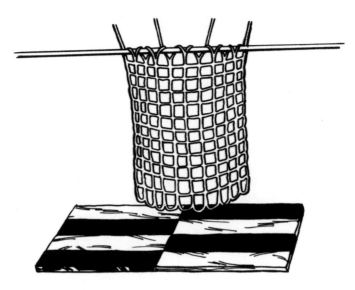

Figure 3.7 Skywriters equipment.

Setup

To prepare for this challenge, set out enough mats or crash pads in the area under the cargo net for safety. Provide a copy of the checklist to the group. Provide paper and pencils so the group can draw plans before climbing onto the cargo net.

Rules and Sacrifices

1. All group members must be on the cargo net and off the floor when the shape is constructed.
2. All group members must be on the same side of the cargo net. (You may wish to modify this rule if your group is large and the cargo net is small.)
3. All the group members must get off the cargo net before constructing the next shape.

There are no sacrifices in this task. However, the teacher must approve the construction of each shape before the next one can be started. If a shape is not approved, the group must make whatever corrections are necessary.

Possible Solutions

The solution to this challenge usually follows a similar pattern for all groups. The group members will position themselves on the cargo net so that each of their bodies becomes a part of the shape being built (see Figure 3.8). Group members may have to assume diagonal, horizontal, or vertical positions. It may be helpful for one group member to remain on the floor until the shape is just about completed. This person can offer suggestions as to the placement or position of individuals, such as whether individuals need to be straighter or more curved in a particular pattern. Once a shape is completed, the group must get the attention of the teacher so that the teacher can approve the shape. All the group members must then come off the cargo net. Students must be careful not to step on one another when descending from their positions.

Figure 3.8 Carrying out the Skywriters challenge.

Conclusion of the Task

At the conclusion of the challenge, the group members will have completed building the designated number of shapes. The group members should sit on the tumbling mats, ready to give each other words of praise or encouragement.

Additions and Variations

Variations may be needed due to the size of your cargo net or the number of members in each group. If your cargo net does not accommodate a large number of students, you may wish to allow group members on both sides of the net, or you may reduce the number of students who construct each shape. If your gym has stall bars on the wall, the challenge can be done on stall bars instead of a cargo net. As mentioned before, this challenge can also be done on the floor or on floor mats for younger children.

Due to the nature of this challenge, group members risk stepping on the hands of their teammates while climbing up and down the cargo net. There needs to be constant communication and encouragement when moving or changing positions on the net so that safety is always foremost.

This challenge looks easier on paper than it is to do on the cargo net. Require the group members to meet some quality standards. Straight lines should look straight, curved lines should bend properly. Do not require students afraid of heights to climb high. Students who frequently climb high need to be reminded to rest or stop if they get tired.

Chapter 4

Intermediate Challenges

Throughout each challenge, kids learn teamwork. As they struggle, fail, reorganize, persevere, and finally succeed, students learn to brainstorm solutions, work together to develop a plan of attack, listen to others, consider others' ideas, and praise and encourage team members.

Island Escape

We cannot teach effective thinking if we as teachers do not understand specific thinking skills. For instance, we should understand problem solving strategy steps: 1. Identify a problem. 2. Clarify the problem. 3. Choose a solution. 4. Carry out the plan. 5. Conclude. 6. Evaluate.

Practical Strategies for the Teaching of Thinking
Barry Beyer

Island Escape is a favorite challenge of many age groups. This task requires a group to transfer themselves across a large open space (the lake) through a series of islands marked by tires. Each island has specific equipment that the group may use. Students must transfer from island to island without skipping islands. Part of the uniqueness of this challenge is that the group must leave the designated equipment at each island when the last person leaves that island. This is our environmentally sound challenge. You may use the resources, but you are not to abuse them.

Description

All group members must travel across the space designated as the lake, stopping at each of the islands. When the group completes the challenge, all the equipment must remain on each island except one scooter. That scooter may remain with the group as they stand on the opposite side of the lake. Group members may not skip islands nor may they send teammates so far ahead that there are empty islands between team members.

Success Criteria

The task is mastered when all the group members have crossed the lake. They may have only one scooter with them. All the rest of the equipment must be on the islands (in or on the tires).

Equipment

You will need five tires for the islands, six scooters, five long jump ropes and five cones (preferably 18-inch cones). You will need a space approximately the length of a standard basketball court and about 10 to 15 feet in width.

Setup

Place the tires in a zigzag fashion (see Figure 4.1) about 15 feet apart. Place one jump rope, one cone, and one scooter in each tire. Place one scooter at the starting line (the edge of the lake). The tires (islands) should be slightly farther apart than the length of the jump ropes. You can use one more or one fewer island depending on the size of your working space.

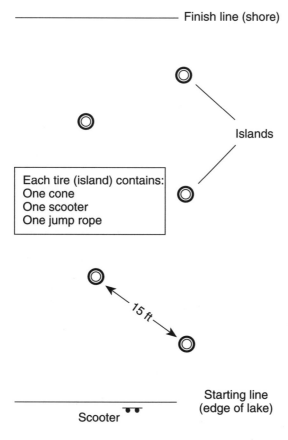

Figure 4.1 Island Escape setup.

Rules and Sacrifices

1. If a group member touches the floor, that person and the person who has advanced the farthest must return to the beginning.
2. If a sacrifice occurs after people are across the lake, one scooter may be brought back to the starting area.
3. If a group member advances two islands ahead so there is an empty island between them and other group members, that person must go back one island before another group member attempts to advance.
4. The tires are not to be moved.
5. No last names or put-downs may be used.

Possible Solutions

The common solution to this task has the group sending one team member to the first island. The team carefully pushes the first person on the scooter provided to (or at least toward) the first tire. That person then pushes the scooter back to the group members on shore. As the team sends a second person, the first person uses the jump rope on the first island to help pull the second person to that island.

At this point, the group may begin to do two things at once. One person can begin making his or her way toward the next island while a scooter is sent back to the starting line. A third person from shore can be sent toward the first island while the two people already there work on getting one of them to the second island (see Figure 4.2).

Figure 4.2   Working on Island Escape.

Group members do not have to advance in any specific order. They may not however, skip islands or leave empty islands between group members.

The cones can be used to help balance team members. They can be used as oars to help propel the scooters to the next island. We have seen students put the cones between their feet and hop to the next island.

Scooters can be tied together to make travel easier. Even though the procession from one island to another is somewhat slow, there is a great deal of interaction and help among group members.

Conclusion of the Task

The challenge will be mastered when all the group members have gone to all the islands and have safely reached the opposite shore. They must leave one scooter, one cone, and one jump rope at each island when they are done.

Additions and Variations

This challenge doesn't need many additions or variations. It incorporates so much interaction that the only necessary variation has been for students who have special physical needs. Usually they may be accommodated by tying scooters together.

You might experiment by adding objects to carry across the lake (wounded group members) or additional obstacles in the lake.

You may decide to rule out hopping on the cones, as it tends to allow group members to work independently without helping one another.

Toxic Waste Transfer

Self-esteem is most likely to be fostered when children have challenging opportunities to build self confidence and esteem through effort, persistence and the gradual accrual of skills, knowledge and appropriate behavior. . . . Learning to deal with setbacks and maintaining the persistence and optimism necessary for childhood's long and gradual road to mastery: These are the real foundations of lasting self-esteem.

All About Me
Lillian Katz

The Toxic Waste Transfer challenge requires the group to transport objects across an open space without directly touching the objects or their container. The group will manipulate a bucket filled with small objects using ropes attached to the bucket.

Description

The group members will form a circle around a 5-gallon bucket. This bucket will have numerous ropes attached to it. The group members must hold onto the end of the ropes. Working together, the group will transport the bucket from one terminal to the other terminal by manipulating the ropes. By manipulating the ropes, the group will transfer the contents of the bucket into another container. If a toxic waste spill occurs, the group must select a toxic waste expert from their group to dress in protective clothing, put the spilled toxic material back into the original bucket, remove the protective clothing, and then continue the transfer process. Each time a new spill occurs, a new group member must be chosen as the toxic waste expert.

Success Criteria

The challenge will be mastered when the group has successfully transferred all the contents of the bucket into the second container.

Equipment

You will need to make a toxic waste transport bucket. Take a 5-gallon bucket and attach 10 to 12 ropes, 8 feet or more in length, to it. You can simply drill holes in the bucket, slip a rope through a hole, and tie a tight knot in the end of the rope (see Figure 4.3). You will need a second bucket or box to act as the disposal container. In addition, you may wish to create a special protective clothing costume. A snowmobile suit or coveralls, boots, hat or helmet, and oversized gloves would make a good costume. You might want to set out two distinctive boundaries for the two containers, such as two tumbling mats, hoops, or bicycle tires. You might also want a box or backpack for the group to carry the protective clothing in. Use colored tape to mark the section of the rope that the students may handle. For example, mark the end of the rope with green tape. Place a red mark 12 inches from the end. Students may hold the rope only between the tape lines.

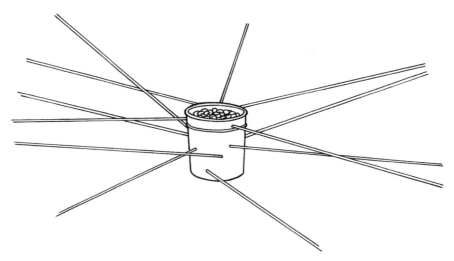

Figure 4.3   Toxic Waste Transfer bucket.

For the toxic waste material, fill the bucket (but not to the very top) with Styrofoam packing peanuts, golf balls, or plastic golf balls.

Setup

Place the bucket with ropes and toxic waste material on the floor approximately 40 to 50 feet from the second container. A distance of three fourths of a gym length would be adequate. Set out the package of protective clothing for the group to carry as well.

Rules and Sacrifices

1. If the toxic waste bucket touches the floor, the entire group must start the task from the beginning.
2. If a group member touches any toxic waste from the transport bucket when not wearing the protective clothing, the group must start the task again.
3. If a group member touches a rope anywhere other than between the tape lines, the group starts again.
4. If the toxic waste expert places the spilled contents into the wrong container, the group must start over.
5. The group cannot continue the process after a toxic spill until the expert has taken off all the protective clothing. The sacrifice is to start from the beginning.
6. No last names or put-downs may be used.

Possible Solutions

There is one basic solution to this challenge. Each group, however, will have to struggle as a team to achieve success. The group members will carefully transport the contents of the toxic waste container by moving together and manipulating the ropes (see Figure 4.4). As they transfer the contents of the first container into the second, they must work slowly and carefully. If a toxic waste spill occurs, the group must be careful not to let the first container touch the floor. One group member must quickly put on the protective clothing (other group members may assist in this process), clean up the spill, and place the spilled material into the first container. The toxic waste expert must then remove the protective gear and join the group in their effort to complete the exchange. If other spills occur, a different group member must serve as the toxic waste expert each time.

Conclusion of the Task

The task is completed when the group members have transferred all the contents of the transport bucket into the second container without any of the material being left on the floor.

Figure 4.4 Working on the Toxic Waste Transfer challenge.

Additions and Variations

You may allow groups to rest the transport bucket on the floor in designated areas (such as inside hula hoops or bicycle tires) if the group needs to reorganize themselves or wait for the toxic waste expert to clean up.

Team-A-Pod

When one door of opportunity closes, another opens. But, so often we look so long at the closed door, we do not see the one which has been opened for us.

Helen Keller

Team-A-Pod was created at one of our workshops held in La Crosse, WI. Group members must physically assist and balance one another while traveling across a designated space. The group will creatively sculpt with their bodies a large millipede-like creature that moves with only a limited number of body parts touching the floor.

The group members will be required to hold onto or lift one another during this challenge. This usually produces a lot of laughter and giggles at first, but it can be a fun challenge requiring strength, intelligence, and cooperation.

We suggest you have each group travel across the designated space more than once. They can also be asked to change their millipede each time they cross the designated space.

Description

The team will move themselves across a 30-foot area with collectively only five body parts in contact with the floor. This challenge is set up for a seven-member team. The number of floor contact points can change depending on the number of team members.

Success Criteria

The challenge is mastered when the team travels from the starting point to the finish point using only the specified number of floor contact points.

Equipment

You will need a flat, matted surface, such as a wrestling room or a 30-foot matted path, and cones or tape to mark the starting and finish lines.

Setup

Lay mats end to end and put cones on mats to designate the starting and finish lines. This challenge does not present safety concerns if the group stays in the designated matted area. Do not allow the group to build an unsafe movable pyramid. You may want to limit the stacking of team members on top of one another.

Rules and Sacrifices

1. If more than the number of specified contact points touches the floor, the entire team must return to the starting line.
2. No last names or put-downs may be used.

Possible Solutions

Teamwork is the solution to this challenge. Members must discuss the strength and flexibility of all group members before attempting to move. The team must move slowly and with cooperation, as in Figure 4.5.

Conclusion of the Task

The group is successful when the entire team crosses the finish line.

Figure 4.5 One solution to Team-A-Pod.

Additions and Variations

This challenge is open to a variety of additions and variations.

- Use scooters or carpet squares that are not considered as points in contact with the floor.
- Create obstacles in the 30-foot path.
- Change the number of contact points.
- Make the number of contact points larger for a younger group.
- Have the group travel to the finish line using a specified number of contact points and back to the starting line with a different number of contact points.

Ship to Shore

Eroding self esteem is much easier than building it. We need to be searchers of strength rather than searchers of weakness.

The Master Teacher, Inc.
Manhattan, KS

In Ship to Shore, the team is stranded on a sinking ship in the ocean. They must devise a way to get back to shore before the ship goes down. You can use a variety of equipment to create different atmospheres as you conduct this challenge. This challenge was created by the Successful Seven at a team-building workshop in Appleton, WI.

Description

Group members will begin with travel equipment on their stranded ship in the middle of the ocean. All team members must travel from the ship to island 1 and stay on island 1 before advancing to island 2. Teammates must stay at island 2 before traveling to shore.

Success Criteria

The challenge is mastered when all group members have traveled from the stranded ship and are safely ashore.

Equipment

You will need three volleyball standards, three auto tires, two scooters, one rope (at least 20 feet long), and one ship (two folded mats pushed together).

Setup

Put each of the three automobile tires over a volleyball standard (see Figure 4.6) and slide it to the base of the standard. Two standards will be islands and the third will be the shore.

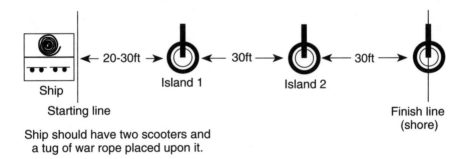

Figure 4.6 Ship to Shore setup.

Secure the volleyball standards so they cannot move or tip over during the challenge. Place all other equipment on the ship along with all teammates. The ship should be behind a starting line about 20 to 30 feet from the first island. The volleyball standards (islands) should be about 30 feet apart. Of course, the islands may have to be placed where the floor anchors are located.

Rules and Sacrifices

1. All group members must reach and remain on island 1 before anyone travels to island 2.
2. All group members must reach and remain on island 2 before traveling to shore.
3. Group members may not touch the water with any part of their bodies.
4. If any rule is broken, the person who broke the rule plus a successful member must return to the ship and start over.
5. No last names or put-downs may be used.

Possible Solutions

Most team members will use the rope and scooters to advance themselves from island to island, as in Figure 4.7. Shipmates must help group members to get off the scooter and onto the island without touching the floor. They then must balance themselves on the island as they prepare to move to the next island.

Figure 4.7   Working on the Ship to Shore challenge.

Conclusion of the Task

At the conclusion of the challenge, all crew members and equipment, except the tires and volleyball standards, will be on the shore.

Additions and Variations

We suggest the following additions and variations:

- Distances from ship to island, island to island, and island to shore may be varied to suit the facility.
- Props could be transported with the group such as fish, treasures, provisions, or life jackets.
- Set a time limit for the crew to reach shore.
- Time the challenge. The next time the group attempts the challenge, they should try to improve their time.
- Put obstacles such as rocks, sharks, or reefs in the ocean.

Plunger Ball

A group becomes a team when all members are sure enough of themselves and their contributions to praise the skills of others.

Anonymous

Plunger Ball requires a group to build a conveyor system in order to transfer basketballs from a designated area through a basketball hoop into a container. The group members must devise a plan to move the balls so that they do not touch the basketballs with their hands. The group members will use certain pieces of equipment to manipulate the basketballs.

Description

Group members must work together to form a conveyor to transport basketballs using five pairs of tinikling poles. The basketballs must travel along the poles toward the designated basketball hoop, and they must stay over the heads of the group members holding the poles. As the ball comes across the last pair of poles, some group members must help to lift the ball onto a tall plunger, using small plungers to guide or lift the ball. The ball will then need to be carefully lifted up to the designated basket, dropped into the hoop, and then caught in a large container resting on the floor. Once the group gets a ball into the receiving cart, they will repeat the procedure with the next ball.

Success Criteria

The task will be completed when all the basketballs have been dropped through the hoop into the large container.

Equipment

You will need five pairs of tinikling poles (8 to 10 feet long), three basketballs, three deck tennis rings on which to place the basketballs, four small bathroom plungers, one plunger mounted onto a 5- to 6-foot mop handle, and a large container such as a custodial cart or large garbage can. If you do not have tinikling poles, use plastic PVC plumbing pipe. Pipe that is 1-1/2 inches in diameter is fine. Use 8- to 10-foot lengths. Plungers can usually be found at discount stores, outlet stores, hardware stores, or full service lumber and remodeling businesses.

Setup

You need a space about three fourths the size of a basketball court. Set the three basketballs onto the deck tennis rings. Place the rings on the free-throw line opposite the basket you will travel toward. Set the poles in pairs lying end-to-end down the center of the basketball court (see Figure 4.8). Set two small plungers at each end of the line of poles. Lay the tall plunger near the designated hoop into which the basketballs must fall. Set the large container under the basket.

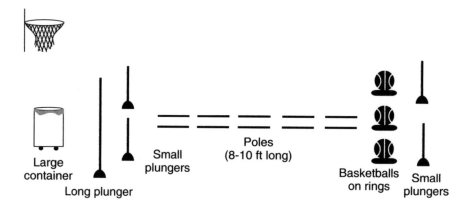

Figure 4.8 Plunger Ball setup.

Rules and Sacrifices

1. If the ball touches the floor, the group must start at the beginning.
2. If the ball touches any part of a group member's body, the ball must go back to the starting position. There is one exception. The ball may roll over the hands of the people holding the poles.

3. A group member may hold only one plunger at a time. If a group member holds onto two or more plungers, the ball must be returned to the beginning position.
4. When the ball goes through the basketball hoop, it must fall into the large container. If it misses, the ball must be returned to the beginning.
5. No one may use put-downs or last names.

Possible Solutions

The most common solution is to have two group members, each holding a small plunger, lift a basketball onto the first pair of poles held by two other group members. The group members holding the poles may be standing, kneeling, or lying on the floor (see Figure 4.9). These people will try to roll the ball along the poles and then transfer the ball to the next set of poles. The two group members with the plungers may help steady or guide the ball as it rolls along the poles. The ball must make its way across all five sets of poles.

As the ball reaches the end of the line, one group member will be holding the tall plunger. Other group members may use the other available plungers to lift or guide the ball onto the tall plunger. The group may then slowly lift the ball toward the basketball hoop. As the ball drops through the hoop, it must land in the designated receiving container. One or more group members may try to manipulate the cart so that the basketball falls into it.

Figure 4.9 Working on the Plunger Ball challenge.

Groups may choose slightly different ways to hold the poles. They may work in pairs so that there are two people per pair of poles. These people may have to set their poles down and pick up another set once the ball is transferred to the adjacent set of poles. Using another method, some group members are actually holding the ends of two different sets of poles, connecting them to create a railroad track effect.

Groups may stand, kneel, or lie on the floor as long as the ball is transferred above their heads from one pair of poles to another.

Conclusion of the Task

The group will have completed the task when all the balls have gone through the basketball hoop and have successfully landed in the receiving cart.

Additions and Variations

The number of balls the groups must transfer is your decision. We recommend three to five basketballs. The challenge becomes more difficult if the group members are required to stand when transferring the balls from one set of poles to another.

You may find additions or variations that meet your needs. Since this challenge requires so much group participation and interaction and is so time consuming, other variations may not be necessary.

Chapter 5

Advanced Challenges

I do not believe that there is any secret or single formula for success, but there are common threads of thought and action that characterize successful people. I do know, from my own experience, that our chance of succeeding is much greater when we organize and take charge of our lives.

Merlin Olson
Quoted in The Edge

Knights of the Around Table

Games that children and adults play, in any situation, usually have highly structured organization and will result in predictable conclusions. Team building, unlike games, devises rules as challenges evolve. The products can be very unpredictable.

Team building has given us the opportunity to meet with many other teachers. Many times these meetings evolve into a lively exchange of team-building ideas. During one of these workshops, Knights of the Around Table was created. It is a very difficult and special challenge. In addition, this challenge is a good lead-up to the Electric Fence from our first book, *Team Building Through Physical Challenges.*

Description

The group must stand behind the starting line, which runs the length of a sturdy table and is positioned 3 feet from the side of the table. The group must transfer all members over, under, and then over the table again without touching the floor. All group members must exit the top of the table beyond the finish line, which runs the length of the table 3 feet from the side opposite the starting line (see Figure 5.1).

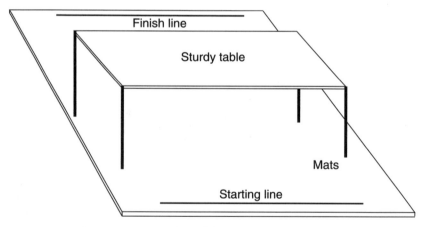

Figure 5.1 Knights of the Around Table setup.

Success Criteria

The challenge will be mastered when all group members have successfully crossed over, then under, and then over the table again and are standing behind the finish line.

Equipment

The only equipment needed for this challenge is a sturdy table, a roll of tape, and two large folding mats. We do not think a folding table will work as the possibility of collapse is greater.

Setup

Place the mats side by side. Set the table on top of the mats. Make sure the table is not wobbly and all the table legs are secure. Tape a starting line 3 feet longer than the table and 3 feet from the side of the table. The finish line should be on the opposite side of the table, 3 feet from that side of the table.

Rules and Sacrifices

1. If a group member touches the floor between the starting line and finish line that person plus a sacrificed person must start over.
2. Once a group member leaves the table and is standing behind the finish line he or she may not get back on the table.
3. Group members standing behind the starting line or the finish line may assist the group member attempting to go around the table, but they may not touch the table. (Depending on the age and ability of your group, you may allow two or three people to touch the table. This makes the challenge much easier.)
4. Negative pressure and put-downs are not allowed.
5. No one may call a teammate by his or her last name.

Possible Solutions

Team success during this challenge will be impossible without a strategy to physically assist all team members. Team members should select the most athletic person to go first, and the team should assist that person as best they can from behind the starting line. Once the first person travels under the table and successfully gets to the top, that person should stay on the top of the table to assist others. Another strategy may be to send two people to the top of the table before any one person attempts to crawl under and over (see Figure 5.2).

Getting someone to the finish line and allowing them to help from that position is helpful. Remember, providing physical assistance is permitted from behind the starting and finish lines as long as the table is not touched by those providing assistance.

Conclusion of the Task

The task is mastered when all team members have traveled over, under, and then over the table again and are standing behind the finish line.

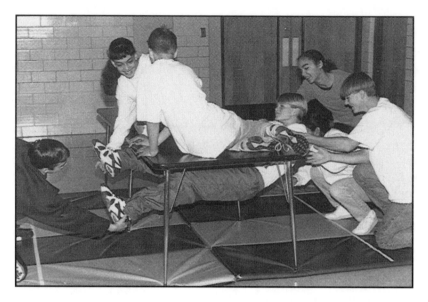

Figure 5.2 Working the Knights of the Around Table challenge.

Additions and Variations

Try the following additions and variations:

- Use a wider table.
- Adjust the distance of the starting and finish lines.
- Have the team attempt to transport a football dummy (injury victim) over, under, and then over the table.
- Put a time limit on the journey.
- Allow other team members to touch the table.

Grand Canyon II

Teamwork is developed by working, playing, and accomplishing goals together.

Grand Canyon II is an advanced challenge. It is one of the favorites of most student groups. It differs from the Grand Canyon challenge in *Team Building Through Physical Challenges* both in its setup and its complexity of teamwork. Group members will travel across an open space from one cliff to another using a climbing rope to swing across the Grand Canyon.

Description

The group will transfer its members from cliff 1 to cliff 2. They will attempt to swing across the open space between the cliffs and land safely on the second cliff. Group members will need to assist one another both in swinging as well as in safe landing. The placement of the rope in relationship to cliff 1 will determine the difficulty level of this challenge.

Success Criteria

The challenge will be mastered when all the group members have safely crossed the Grand Canyon and are standing on cliff 2.

Equipment

You will need one climbing rope for swinging. Two large crash pads will be needed for the two cliffs. (If you do not have crash pads, you may safely stack tumbling mats to create the two cliffs.) Additional mats will be needed between the cliffs as well as over any floor space where the group may be working. When in doubt, mat the area.

Setup

Set the first cliff almost directly under the climbing rope. (The rope should be about 1 to 2 feet away from the front edge of the cliff.) The closer the rope is to the cliff, the more difficult you will make the challenge. Set the second cliff far enough away so that a person reaching the second cliff must stretch to make it onto that cliff. This distance will vary depending on your gym space and the length of your rope. Cover the floor area with tumbling mats. Place additional mats around the cliffs in the event someone falls off the cliff. If a cliff is near a wall, be sure to place crash pads against that wall, so that students who may swing into the wall will not get hurt. See Figure 5.3.

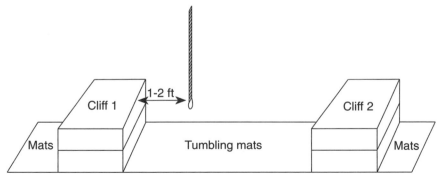

Figure 5.3 Grand Canyon setup.

Rules and Sacrifices

1. If a group member touches the floor (Grand Canyon), that person and one successful person must return to cliff 1.
2. If a group member falls off a cliff onto the floor, that person and one successful person must go back to cliff 1.
3. No one may use last names or put-downs.

Possible Solutions

Although this challenge has one basic solution, each group will find their own challenge to be unique.

The group will begin by trying to find one person who can make it across the canyon and safely land on cliff 2. This process often can take a while. The group will have to find a method to efficiently swing group members. After some make it to cliff 2, the group members there will have to help others stretch and land on that cliff (see Figure 5.4). The group will also have to wisely choose the last person to swing across. The last person will have to attempt to swing across without the benefit of a push or other help from the first side. Balance will be important as the group works from both cliffs. Carelessness will result in people stepping off the cliffs, which requires a sacrifice. In addition, the group will have to make good choices in their sacrifices. They should not sacrifice people who were difficult to get across the canyon, if at all possible.

Figure 5.4 Working on the Grand Canyon challenge.

Conclusion of the Task

The challenge will be completed when all the group members have successfully made it across the canyon. They must all be standing on cliff 2, and they will be cheering wildly.

Additions and Variations

The difficulty of this challenge will be determined by the placement of the rope and the distance between the cliffs. Please make this task tough. The group should struggle. If you have a group member who needs a special adaptation, feel free to make an exception to the rules. A tire placed in the canyon could be used as a resting place or stepping stone. But give this adaptation to those who need it, not the entire group.

Arachnophobia

Violence in our schools is a growing concern for everyone involved in education. Team building can reduce the incidence of violence by teaching students to encourage and praise one another.

Arachnophobia is another challenge invented at one of our team-building workshops in La Crosse, WI. The challenge here is for a group to work themselves through a horizontal spiderweb without touching any part of the web. This is a difficult challenge that requires a great deal of physical help from teammates. You may want to hang up some Halloween spiders from the web to create a more vivid visual image.

Description

All group members must travel from one end of the web to the other—without touching the web or any supports that hold the web. Group members must travel over each web strand. They are not to travel under the web.

Success Criteria

The challenge is mastered when all group members have successfully crossed the web without breaking any rules.

Equipment

You will need two high balance beams or other study supports, such as heavy tables, chairs, or volleyball standards; 20 to 30 yards of elastic string or yarn; and three large, flat mats.

Setup

The team will create a series of geometric shapes of varying sizes, but large enough for at least three team members to fit inside the shape. The supporting standards need to be parallel and about 8 feet apart. The web should be about 16 feet long and about waist-high on the tallest team member (see Figure 5.5). Place mats below the entire spiderweb area.

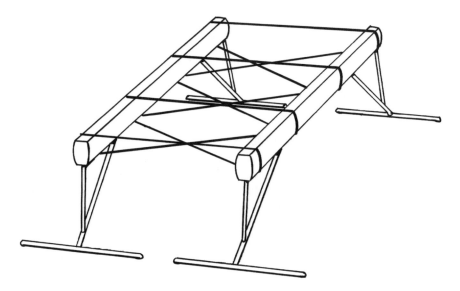

Figure 5.5   Arachnophobia web.

Rules and Sacrifices

1. All group members must start at one end of the web on the mat.
2. Team members may not touch any web supports or the web itself.
3. Group members may never travel under the web.
4. If a rule is broken, the group must sacrifice the one who made the mistake plus one or more successful members as needed for assistance reentering the web.

Possible Solutions

The group must plan the best possible route through the web and decide who is best able to assist and who is the most agile. Then the team should start by lifting one member over the first thread of the web. Once that is accomplished, there will be help on both sides of the web to assist teammates over. Remember, the open spaces should be big enough to allow only three people inside, so some will have to leave the first space and proceed to the second and third before other teammates can start (see Figure 5.6). Getting the last person inside presents the greatest difficulty. The last person could jump over with the support of teammates, or two teammates could lift him or her over the web strand.

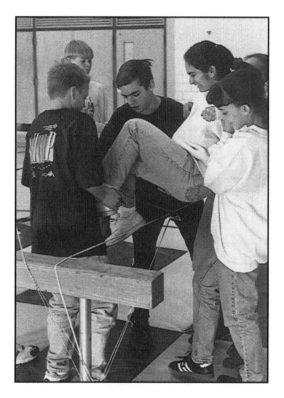

Figure 5.6   Working on the Arachnophobia challenge.

Conclusion of the Task

At the conclusion of the task, all group members will be standing on the exit side of the web on the matted area.

Additions and Variations

Try these variations:

- Raise or lower the height of the web.
- Establish a time limit.
- Hang spiders from the web—participants may not touch spiders.

Bridge Across the Amazon

Many times, the first things we eliminate from our children's lives are the very things that built character in our own lives: struggle, failure, deferred gratification. Let your students experience these building blocks.

Bridge Across the Amazon is a new twist on an old idea. The Mindful Doers of Appleton, WI, created this challenge. Bridge Across the Amazon takes elements from Bridge Over the Raging River and Grand Canyon from *Team Building Through Physical Challenges* and creates a different and less stable working area.

Description

The team must transfer themselves from ledge A to ledge B. The ledges can be built from folded tumbling mats. Put two or three together to make stable ledges. Members must build a bridge on the river in order to get from ledge A to ledge B. This is made more challenging because the river is made out of high-jump landing pads or gymnastic crash pads. This provides a very unstable river-like surface that is very difficult to cross.

Success Criteria

The challenge is mastered when all group members have safely crossed the river without falling in. All members plus all bridge-building materials must be on ledge B at the conclusion of the challenge.

Equipment

You will need crash pads or high-jump or pole-vault pads. The number of pads depends on how long you want to make the river. You will also need two two-by-fours; four auto tires; a climbing rope; two folded mats; and two large, flat mats.

Setup

Set the crash pads or high-jump mats end to end. Position the climbing rope over the rapids—the area between the last crash pad and ledge B. Do not make this distance more than 6 feet. Make sure a flat mat is under the climbing rope (see Figure 5.7).

Rules and Sacrifices

1. All team members must travel over the river without falling in. If someone touches the river, that person plus a sacrificed teammate must start over.

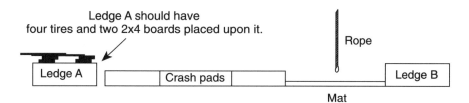

Ledge A should have
four tires and two 2x4 boards placed upon it.

Rope

Ledge A

Crash pads

Ledge B

Mat

Figure 5.7 Bridge Across the Amazon setup.

2. The two-by-fours may not rest in the river with team members on it. The two-by-fours must be supported by the tires.
3. All bridge-building materials must be brought across the river.
4. No last names or put-downs can be used.

Possible Solutions

The team must construct a bridge across the river using the two-by-fours and tires. The unstable surface makes balancing much more difficult. Team members must physically assist teammates as well as move slowly and cautiously (see Figure 5.8). The climbing rope can be used to swing across the rapids to ledge B.

Figure 5.8 Working on the Bridge Across the Amazon challenge.

Conclusion of the Task

The task is completed when all team members have crossed the river and all bridge-building materials are safely on ledge B.

Additions and Variations

We suggest the following additions and variations:

- Add equipment to be carried.
- Add or delete bridge-building equipment, such as add another two-by-four or delete a tire or the climbing rope.
- Set a time limit for the river crossing.

Raiders of the Lost Jewel

Many children do not have a positive family environment, or they may be exposed to negative peer pressure. Team building gives each person a sense of belonging to a group. Team building can make each person feel better about themselves as well as others.

Raiders of the Lost Jewel is yet another task that was conceived at one of our team-building workshops. This challenge can be quite difficult; at the same time, it allows you to make quite a few adaptations in regard to the equipment you use, the paths you create, and rules you use.

Description

The group must work together to journey across an uncharted territory to find and retrieve the Lost Jewel. Once the group reaches the Jewel, they must take it off its stand without touching it with their hands. They must then transport the Jewel and the stand back to their home base. Team members must use plungers or deck tennis rings to move their scooter. They must not touch the floor with any part of their bodies.

Success Criteria

Using all the group members, the team will bring the Jewel, the stand, and all the other equipment used in the journey back to the designated home base.

Equipment

The equipment needed for this challenge will vary slightly depending on the availability of materials at your facility and how you wish to set up the task (see the "Additions and Variations" for further discussion). For our description, we recommend the following pieces of equipment: a cage ball (the Jewel); a stand for the cage ball such as a stack of tires, garbage can, or foam hexagon; a few hurdles for obstacles (manufactured hurdles or two 18-inch cones and a plastic bar); plungers; deck tennis rings; a scooter for each team member plus one extra scooter; and four two-by-four boards, 6 to 8 feet long (two per riverboat).

Setup

Place the hurdles randomly throughout the working area (see Figure 5.9). If you wish, you can place a deck tennis ring or plunger by each hurdle to be retrieved by the group if they need more equipment. Place the cage ball on the stand from one half to three quarters of the working space away from the home base. Place the boards, scooters, and plungers at the home base.

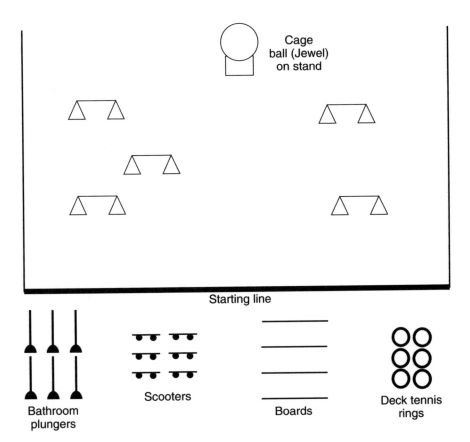

Figure 5.9 Raiders of the Lost Jewel setup.

Rules and Sacrifices

1. Team members may not touch the Jewel with their hands.
2. The Jewel may not touch the floor.
3. Team members may not touch the floor with any part of their bodies.
4. Team members may not touch a hurdle.
5. No last names or put-downs may be used.
6. If any rule is broken, the group must return to the home base and begin again.

Possible Solutions

The group will use the scooters to begin their journey to the Lost Jewel. They will use the plungers and deck tennis rings as oars or paddles to move themselves across the floor.

Once they get to the Jewel, they will have to lift it using their plungers. Some group members may need to support the Jewel while others paddle back. Some members may need to paddle with one hand and support the Jewel with a plunger in their other hand. In addition, one or more of the group members will need to carry the Jewel's stand. See Figure 5.10.

One person usually follows the team behind the Jewel to keep the Jewel from falling backward.

Figure 5.10   Working on the Raiders of the Lost Jewel challenge.

Conclusion of the Task

The group members will have mastered the challenge when they have success-fully returned the Jewel to the home base and set it on the stand without the Jewel touching the floor.

Additions and Variations

The challenge will be more or less difficult depending on the size of the cage ball you use. We use a 4-foot diameter cage ball for our challenges, and it is difficult. A very large beach ball will work, but it will make the challenge easy.

We suggest using at least four more plungers than you have group members. If you do not have plungers, use deck tennis rings. Two tools per group member should be the maximum (two plungers, one plunger and one deck tennis ring, or two deck tennis rings).

You may allow the group members to let the Jewel balance against their heads. With younger groups, you might allow them to paddle with their hands touching the floor. Again, the size of the ball you use for the Jewel will make a tremendous difference in the difficulty of this challenge.

You might change the sacrifice from everyone starting over to the group losing a piece of equipment, or having the person who made the error and one other team member (such as the person farthest ahead) go back to the home base. These two members would then have to work their way back to the group before the group could go forward.

Appendix A

Team Report Card

Instructor Preparation Form

The Great Communicator Examples

Skywriters Checklist Example

Team Report Card

1. How did our team involve everyone in solving the challenge?

2. Did our team use negative pressure or put-downs during the challenge?

3. Did we listen to one another and use ideas that we shared?

4. How many and which team members used praise phrases or positive encouragement?

5. What were some of the praise phrases used?

Instructor Preparation Form

Challenge: _____

Level of difficulty:

Equipment needed:

To master the challenge:

Rules and sacrifices:

Variations:

Safety considerations:

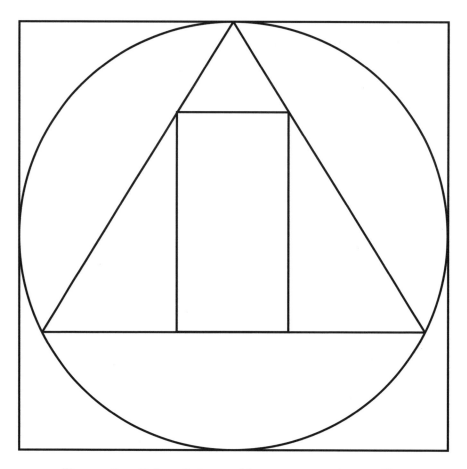

Describe this picture. You may not use the following words:

Circle
Square
Triangle
Rectangle
Arc

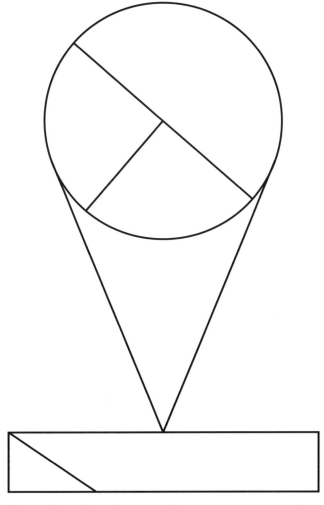

Describe this picture. You may not use the
following words:

Circle
Square
Triangle
Rectangle
Arc

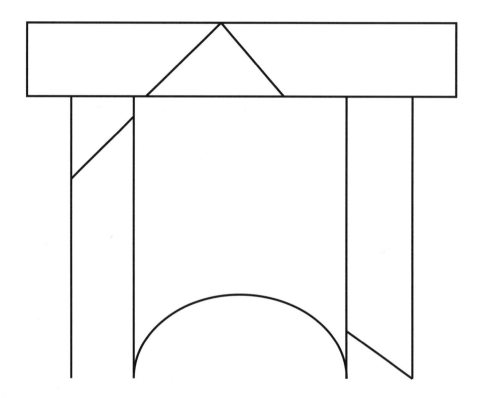

Describe this picture. You may not use the following words:

Circle
Square
Triangle
Rectangle
Arc

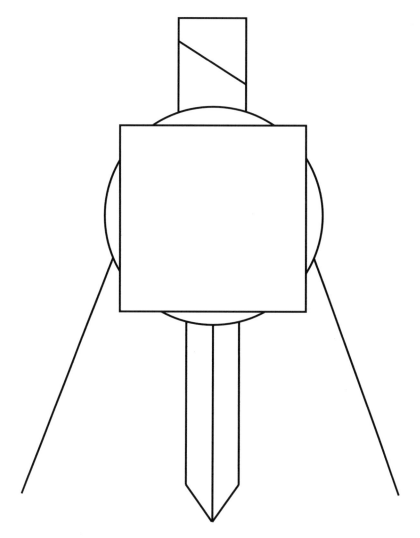

Describe this picture. You may not use the
following words:

Circle
Square
Triangle
Rectangle

Skywriters Checklist Example

□ ___ + ___

○ ___ ⬓ ___

△ ___ ⬡ ___

Appendix B

Challenge Cards

Organizer Cards

Challenge Card | The Great Communicator

Equipment

Each group member will need a pencil and one piece of paper per drawing. The Great Communicator will be given a picture to describe and one clipboard on which to put the picture.

Starting Position

The group will sit in a semicircle or random space in front of the Great Communicator.

Our Challenge

Each group member will attempt to draw a picture from the descriptions given by the Great Communicator.

Rules and Sacrifices

There are no sacrifices in this challenge. The Great Communicator is expected not to use the following terms: circle, square, rectangle, triangle, or certain other shape names. The group members may not ask the Great Communicator any questions.

The Great Communicator |

Questions

1. What equipment do we use?
2. What is our starting position?
3. What can we ask the Great Communicator?
4. What terms must the Great Communicator avoid using?

Caution: Construction Zone

Equipment

One to four blindfolds will be needed. A construction puzzle or puzzles will be provided by the teacher.

Starting Position

The sighted group members will mix up the puzzle. The blindfolded group members will sit in the construction zone.

Our Challenge

The blindfolded construction workers will assemble the puzzle while receiving verbal instructions from the sighted group members. The blindfolded workers must not remove their blindfolds until the puzzle is assembled.

Rules and Sacrifices

1. Only the blindfolded team members may touch the puzzle pieces. If sighted members touch the puzzle pieces, the group must mix up the puzzle again and start from the beginning.
2. The sighted group members may not physically touch the blindfolded group members. If they do, the group must mix up the puzzle and start from the beginning.
3. No one may use put-downs or last names.

Caution: Construction Zone | Organizer Card

Questions

1. What equipment will we use?
2. What happens if a sighted group member touches a blindfolded construction worker?
3. What happens if a sighted group member touches a puzzle piece?
4. When can the blindfolded construction workers remove their blindfolds?

Challenge Card

The Riverboat

Equipment

Two folded tumbling mats, two small tires, two jump ropes.

Starting Position

All group members begin at one end of the gym.

Our Challenge

Using the designated equipment, the group will travel from one end of the gym to the other end without touching the floor (the river).

Rules and Sacrifices

1. If a group member touches the floor, the entire group must go back to the starting position.
2. All the equipment must be brought across the river.
3. The mats must remain folded. If the riverboat falls apart, the group starts over.
4. If the mat crashes to the floor (the riverboat explodes) and makes a loud noise, the group returns to the starting line.

The Riverboat

Questions

1. Where are the beginning and end lines of the river?
2. What happens if someone touches the river?
3. What must we do with the equipment?
4. What happens if the mat crashes to the floor?
5. What happens if the mat falls apart while we are moving it?

The Swamp Machine

Equipment

Four standard tumbling mats (two for each island). One 6-by-12-foot mat for the swamp machine. A large, open space for the swamp.

Starting Position

All group members must begin on island 1. The swamp machine will also be on that island.

Our Challenge

The task will be completed when all the group members are standing on island 2 along with the swamp machine.

Rules and Sacrifices

1. If a group member touches the floor (swamp), that person and one successful person must go back to island 1.
2. If the swamp machine falls apart, there is no sacrifice. However, if the group members inside cannot repair the swamp machine, the entire group must return to island 1.
3. No group member may take more than two consecutive trips across the swamp. If one does, that person and one person from island 2 must return to island 1.
4. There must always be from two to four teammates in the swamp machine as it crosses the swamp. If there are less than two or more than four, the entire group must begin the task again from the beginning.
5. No one may use last names or put-downs.

The Swamp Machine

Questions

1. What happens if a group member touches the floor?
2. What happens if the swamp machine falls apart?
3. What happens if we cannot repair the swamp machine while it is in the swamp?
4. What happens if a group member takes more than two consecutive trips across the swamp?
5. How many group members must travel in the swamp machine?

Equipment

A hanging cargo net, tumbling mats or crash pads under the net for safety, a checklist of shapes to be constructed, and paper and pencils for drawing plans.

Starting Position

All the group members will stand on the mats next to the cargo net. All group members will start on the same side of the net.

Our Challenge

Using all the group members, the team must construct the designated number of shapes assigned by the teacher.

Rules and Sacrifices

1. All the group members must be on the cargo net and off the floor when the shape is done.
2. All the group members must be on the same side of the cargo net.
3. All the group members must get off the cargo net before a new shape is constructed.

There are no sacrifices in this task. However, the teacher must approve a shape before another shape can be built.

Skywriters

Questions

1. What equipment will we use?
2. Do we all have to be on the cargo net?
3. How many people have to be part of each shape we make?
4. How many shapes will we build?
5. What do we do after the teacher approves our shape?
6. What are the sacrifices in this challenge?

Challenge Card   Island Escape

Equipment
Five tires (to remain stationary), five 18-inch cones, six scooters, five long jump ropes.

Starting Position
All the group members will begin at one end of the gym.

Our Challenge
The group must travel from island to island until all group members make it across the lake. We must also leave one scooter, one cone, and one jump rope at each island after the last person leaves that island.

Rules and Sacrifices
1. If a group member touches the floor, that person and the person who has advanced the farthest must return to the beginning.
2. If a sacrifice occurs after people are across the lake, a scooter may be brought back to the start.
3. If a group member advances two islands ahead of anyone else, that person must go back one island before another group member attempts to advance.
4. The tires are not to be moved.
5. Group members may not skip an island.

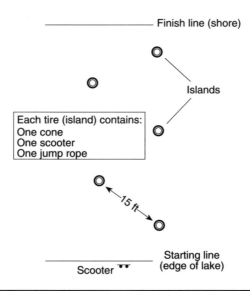

Island Escape

Questions

1. What happens if someone touches the floor?
2. Can we move the tires?
3. Can we skip islands?
4. What must we leave at each island as the last group member leaves that island?

              Toxic Waste Transfer

Equipment

There will be two containers: one with ropes attached and filled with toxic waste material, the other without ropes. In addition, there will be a container with a work suit, boots, gloves, and a hat or helmet.

Starting Position

The group members will stand around the first container, holding onto the ends of the ropes (some group members may have more than one rope).

Our Challenge

The task is completed when the group has transferred all the material from the first container into the second container without leaving any material on the floor.

Rules and Sacrifices

1. If the toxic waste container touches the floor, the entire group must start the task from the beginning.
2. If a group member touches any toxic waste from the first container without wearing the protective clothing, the group must start the task again.
3. If a toxic waste spill occurs, only the toxic waste expert (chosen by the group) can clean it up.
4. If the toxic waste expert places the spilled contents into the second container, the group must go back to the starting place.
5. The group cannot continue the process after a toxic waste cleanup until the expert has taken off all the protective clothing. The sacrifice is to start from the beginning.
6. The ropes may not touch the floor. If they do, the group must start from the beginning.
7. No one may touch the rope between the red tape mark and the container. If this happens, the group must return to the beginning.
8. No last names or put-downs may be used.

Toxic Waste Transfer

Questions

1. What happens if the toxic waste container touches the floor?
2. What happens if someone touches any toxic waste material without wearing the protective clothing?
3. In which container must we place any spilled material?
4. What happens if we touch a rope between the red mark and container?
5. What happens if the rope touches the floor?

Equipment

Enough mats laid end to end to provide a 30-foot padded runway, four cones to mark starting and finish lines. If cones are not available, use tape lines.

Starting Position

All team members will be standing behind the starting line.

Our Challenge

The seven-member group must safely travel the 30-foot length with only five team body parts touching the floor. The group may not form movable pyramids or stack too many members on top of one another.

Rules and Sacrifices

1. If more than the correct number of body parts touch the floor, then the entire team must start over.
2. No last names or put-downs may be used.

Team-A-Pod

Questions

1. What equipment do we need?
2. What happens if more than five team body parts touch the floor between the start and finish line?
3. Can we build pyramids?
4. Where will we be when our challenge is completed?

Equipment

Three volleyball standards, three auto tires, two scooters, one long rope (at least 20 feet long), two folded mats pushed together.

Starting Position

All group members will be on the ship, behind the starting line. All the equipment except the volleyball standards and auto tires will also be on the ship.

Our Challenge

All group members must travel from their stranded ship and try to get to the shore about 60 feet away. Team members may not touch the floor with any part of their bodies. No team member may move to another island without all team members reaching the previous island. All group members and all equipment must be on the shore at the conclusion of the task.

Rules and Sacrifices

1. All group members must reach and remain on island 1 before anyone travels to island 2.
2. All group members must reach and remain on island 2 before traveling to shore.
3. Group members may not touch the floor with any part of their bodies.
4. If any rule is broken, the person who broke the rule plus one successful person must return to the ship and start over.
5. No last names or put-downs may be used.

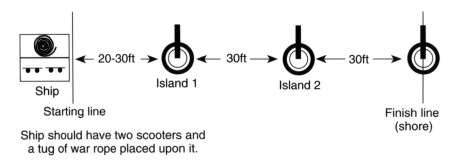

Ship to Shore

Questions

1. What equipment will we use?
2. What happens if anyone touches the floor between the ship and the shore?
3. Can we leave the first island before everyone is there?
4. What happens if we use last names or put-downs?
5. Where will we be when our journey is over?

Equipment

Five pairs of poles, three basketballs, three deck tennis rings, four bathroom plungers, one plunger mounted on a 5- to 6-foot pole such as a mop handle, and a large container such as a custodial cart.

Starting Position

The group members will start near the place where the basketballs are lying.

Our Challenge

The group must transfer each basketball across the five pairs of poles to the basket at the far end of the basketball court. Then they must transfer the ball onto the tall plunger, through the basket, and into the large container. While rolling the ball across the poles, the ball must be over the heads of the people manipulating the poles.

Rules and Sacrifices

1. If the ball touches the floor, the group must start again at the beginning.
2. If the ball touches any part of a group member's body, the ball must go back to the starting position. There is one exception. The ball may roll over the hands of the people holding the poles.
3. Group members may hold only one plunger at a time. If a group member holds two plungers, the ball must be returned to the beginning position.
4. When the ball goes through the basket, it must fall into the large container. If it misses, the group must start again.
5. No one may use last names or put-downs.

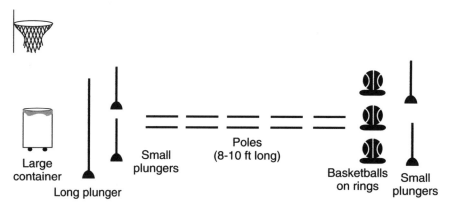

Plunger Ball

Questions

1. Where is our starting position?
2. To which basket do we transfer the basketballs?
3. What do we use to lift the basketballs?
4. What happens if the basketballs touch the floor?
5. What happens if the basketballs touch any part of our bodies?
6. What is the exception to question 5?
7. What do we use to lift the ball into the basket?
8. Do the poles have to be used above our heads?
9. How many plungers can each group member hold at a time?

Knights of the Around Table

Equipment

A sturdy table big enough to crawl under without brushing table legs. The table should be at least 5 to 6 feet in length. Two tape strips to mark starting and finish lines.

Starting Position

All group members will start from behind the starting line located 3 feet from the side of the table.

Our Challenge

All team members must cross over the top, climb under, and again cross over the top of the table without touching the floor. All team members must finish behind the finish line.

Rules and Sacrifices

1. Group members may not touch the floor between the starting and finish lines. If this rule is broken, the person who broke the rule plus one sacrificed person must start over.
2. Group members standing behind the starting or finish line may assist the group member on the table, but they may not touch the table while assisting. If this rule is broken it will again require a one-plus-one sacrifice.
3. Once a group member leaves the table and is standing behind the finish line, he or she may not get back on the table.
4. Negative pressure and put-downs are not allowed.
5. No one may call a teammate by his or her last name. If this rule or rule 4 is broken, the person who broke the rule plus a sacrifice must start over.

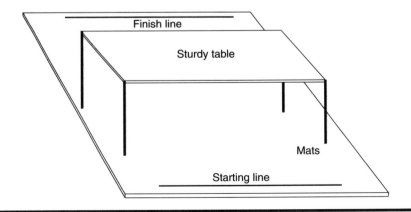

Knights of the Around Table | Organizer Card

Questions

1. What equipment will we use?
2. What happens if anyone touches the floor between the starting and finish lines?
3. What happens if anyone who is standing behind the starting or finish line touches the table?
4. If you get off the top of the table and make it to the finish line, can you get back on the top of the table?
5. What happens if negative pressure, put-downs, or last names are used?

Equipment

One climbing rope for swinging. Crash pads for cliffs. Mats to cover the floor space.

Starting Position

The group members will all begin by standing on cliff 1.

Our Challenge

The task will be completed when all the group members have crossed the Grand Canyon and are standing on cliff 2.

Rules and Sacrifices

1. If a group member touches the floor (Grand Canyon), that person and one successful person must return to cliff 1.
2. If a group member falls off a cliff and touches the floor, that person and one successful person must go back to cliff 1.
3. No one may use last names or put-downs.

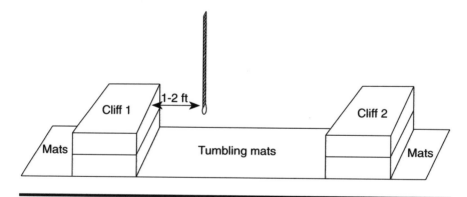

Grand Canyon II

Questions

1. Where is the Grand Canyon?
2. What happens if someone touches the Grand Canyon?
3. What happens if someone falls off a cliff?
4. Where will we be when we are done?
5. What will we be doing when the challenge is complete?

Equipment

Two long tables or two high balance beams. Several folding mats and at least 60 feet of elastic string or yarn.

Starting Position

All team members will start at one end of the spider web.

Our Challenge

The team must get everyone from one end of the spider web to the other. All team members must go over sections of the web, and no more than three group members may be in one section of the web at a time.

Rules and Sacrifices

1. No team member may touch any part of the web or side supports.
2. No more than three group members may be in any section of the web at a time.
3. No one may crawl under the web.
4. No put-downs or last names may be used.
5. If any of these rules are broken, the person who broke the rule plus one or more successful members must start over.

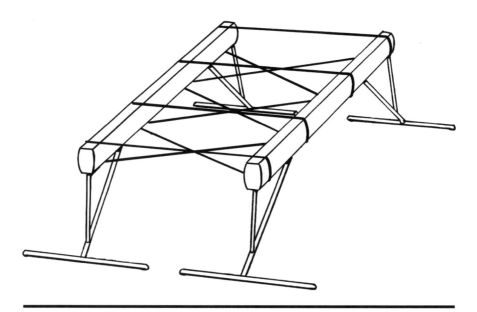

Arachnophobia

Questions

1. Where will we be when we are ready to start?
2. What is our challenge?
3. What happens if anyone touches the web or side support?
4. Can anyone travel under the web?
5. What happens if anyone uses a put-down or last name?
6. Where will we be when our task is over?

Bridge Across the Amazon

Equipment

Four or five crash pads or several high-jump or pole-vault pads; climbing rope; two two-by-fours; four auto tires; two folded mats; and two large, flat mats.

Starting Position

All team members begin on ledge A.

Our Challenge

Using the designated equipment the team will travel from ledge A to ledge B without falling in the river.

Rules and Sacrifices

1. Team members may not touch any part of the river with their bodies. If someone does, that person plus a sacrificed person must start over.
2. The two-by-fours may not rest in the river with team members on it. The two-by-fours must be supported by the tires.
3. All bridge-building materials must be brought across the river to ledge B.
4. No negative pressure, put-downs, or last names can be used. If they are, then the offender plus a sacrificed person must start over.

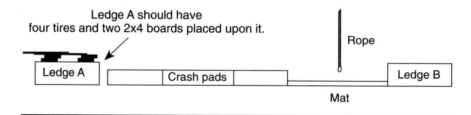

Bridge Across the Amazon

Questions

1. Where are the starting and ending points in this challenge?
2. What happens if anyone touches the river?
3. What happens if someone uses a put-down or a last name?
4. Where will all the equipment be at the end of the challenge?

Raiders of the Lost Jewel

Equipment

You can build two river rafts. They can be made from scooters and 6- to 8-foot lengths of two-by-six boards, or you can use individual scooters for group members. You will be given enough plungers to use as paddles. Plungers will also be used to lift the Jewel. If plungers are not available, you might use deck tennis rings. A 4-foot cage ball will be used as the Lost Jewel. (The Jewel should sit up on a stand such as a stack of four or five tires.)

Starting Position

The group members will begin at a starting line at one end of the gymnasium opposite the Lost Jewel.

Our Challenge

The task will be completed when the group has brought the Lost Jewel and its stand back across the starting line.

Rules and Sacrifices

1. If a group member falls off the river raft or touches the river with his or her body, the group must return to the starting line.
2. If the Lost Jewel touches the floor, the group must begin the task over.
3. If the Lost Jewel is touched by any body part other than a group member's head, the group must start the task over.
4. No one may use last names or put-downs.

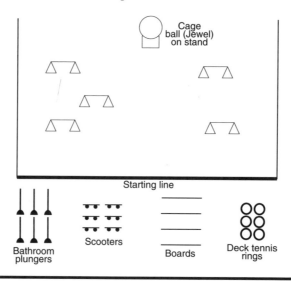

Raiders of the Lost Jewel

| Organizer Card |

Questions

1. What equipment do we get?
2. What happens if one of us touches the floor with any part of our body?
3. What can we use to transport the Jewel?
4. What happens if the Jewel touches the floor?
5. What do we use to propel the river rafts?

About the Authors

Dan Midura   **Don Glover**

Dan Midura, MEd, has taught physical education since 1970. He's the elementary physical education coordinator for the Roseville Minnesota Area School District. Dan is also an adjunct faculty member at Bethel College in St. Paul, Minnesota and at the University of Wisconsin, La Crosse.

Dan received his master's degree in physical education from the University of Minnesota. He received Minnesota's 1994 Teacher of the Year Award for elementary physical education, and the President's Award for Service to the Minnesota Association of Health, Physical Education, Recreation and Dance (MAHPERD).

Dan has published articles on elementary education and held clinics at numerous state and national workshops and conventions. He is a member of the United States Physical Association (USPE), MAHPERD, the American Alliance for Health, Physical Education, Recreation and Dance (AAHPERD), the Council on Physical Education for Children (COPEC), and the National Association for Sport and Physical Education (NASPE).

Don Glover, MS, has taught physical education (including adapted physical education) since 1967 at the preschool, elementary, secondary, and postsecondary levels. He is the developmental adapted physical education coordinator in the White Bear Lake School District.

Don received his master's degree in physical education from Winona State University. He has received awards as the 1981 Minnesota Teacher of the Year and the 1989 Adapted Physical Education Teacher of the Year.

Don has published numerous magazine and journal articles on physical education and sport and has been a clinician at more than 100 workshops and clinics. He is a member of USPE, MAHPERD, AAHPERD, COPEC, NASPE, and the Minnesota Education Association.

Don and Dan are the co-authors of *Team Building Through Physical Challenges*.

*You'll find
other outstanding
physical education resources at*

www.humankinetics.com

In the U.S. call

1-800-747-4457

Australia ....(08) 8277-1555
Canada.............................(800) 465-7301
Europe .... +44 (0) 113-278-1708
New Zealand ....(09) 309-1890

HUMAN KINETICS
The Information Leader in Physical Activity
P.O. Box 5076 • Champaign, IL 61825-5076 USA